Dedicated to the individuals and organizations
who have allowed me to join them on their
journey to creating their future.

Cover design by Jacob Voigt
jacobvoigt.com

ISBN: 978-0-9885821-4-9

JARED NICHOLS Presents

RETHINKING YOUR NEXT QUARTER (CENTURY)

HOW TO CREATE CONTINUOUS GROWTH
AND ENSURE FUTURE RELEVANCE

With foreword by Glen Hiemstra:
Author of Turning the Future into Revenue

THE
JARED NICHOLS GROUP
empowering organizations to shape the future

Praise for **RETHINKING YOUR NEXT QUARTER (CENTURY)**

"The principles that Jared presents in this book have radically changed my perspective about the future. Having personally worked through this process with Jared, I have greater clarity and confidence about the opportunities and possibilities for my own future and for the future of our organization. This is a must read for the 21st Century leader."

— Rod Nease, SVP Operational Excellence, Sunbelt Rentals, Inc.

"The skills that Jared can teach and enhance are extremely valuable to any business. I have realized that the purpose of strategic foresight is not to predict the future, but rather to identify several potential future outcomes and better prepare for them. His process allows for the facts to emerge to the top and drive sensible decisions."

— Mark Gould, CFO, Mast General Store, Inc.

"When you start to learn more about where you should be going, paradigms that need to shift or change, it helps you to build more confidence in the direction you decide to go, and ultimately helps you produce a real workable strategic vision for a more profitable future. This is a must read for business planners, business owners, management teams and their CEO's. 5 stars."

— Shane Snively, CEO, Abiding Wealth Advisors

"We tend to be in a "status quo default mode" all of the time and Jared takes you out of that mindset very quickly and effectively. This book is easy to read, highly relevant, challenging, and motivating all at once."

— Glenn Love, Development Director, CCM

CONTENTS

FOREWORD

Peter Drucker, the great management professor, once wrote that given the speed at which the world is changing, any business that does not stop to deeply reconsider its fundamental direction every few years is not acknowledging the reality in which they live. The problem is that when organizations engage in strategic planning, they tend not do this kind of fundamental exploration of their long-range direction. Instead they conduct a routine exercise in which they add to or subtract a bit from their traditional goals and call it a plan.

Yet, if an organization wishes to be more effective in deep strategic foresight, they may not have clear ideas on how to do that. This book, Rethinking Your Next Quarter Century, is a very useful introduction for any organization interested in how they might go about longer range strategic thinking. The book offers three distinct concepts in digestible and applicable form.

First, we learn how to adopt a futures perspective that shifts us from being reactive to proactive. Next, comes a simple framework for scanning future trends and issues, called the STEEP Model. The information generated with the STEEP model can then be applied using the technique of scenario building. This provides an opportunity to fundamentally reconsider organization strategies. Examples and fill-in questions throughout the book provide practical tools that you can actually use.

Jared Nichols, the author, is one of a growing cadre of young, academically trained futurists available to help enterprises achieve this kind of foresight and deep thinking. Trained in the use of the latest and best futuring tools, Jared has provided a powerful strategic planning guide.

Jared has done one more thing, something bold, in the title of the book particularly. American organizations especially are hesitant to consider a future beyond a few years. This is partly because we know how fast change is indeed happening, but more so because our management has been trained to think in three-year planning segments, perhaps five years at the most. Beyond that the world seems too nebulous. Yet, there is great utility in taking a very long-term view from time to time, even a quarter century as Jared suggests. Why? The further out you look, the more creative space is available to really ask how things could be different and what you should be doing and why. It is in this creative space that you may find the near term breakthroughs that you hope for when you begin a planning effort.

Glen Hiemstra
CEO and Founder – Futurist.com
Author of *Turning the Future Into Revenue*

ABOUT THE AUTHOR

Jared Nichols is a deep futures strategist, executive advisor, speaker, and coach. He provides the tools to help leaders and organizations gain competitive advantage, seize new market opportunities, drive in new revenue, and increase profits. As one of the few people in the world to hold a Masters Degree in Strategic Foresight, Jared is sought out by leaders, organizations, and entrepreneurs to help them identify and create their long-term successful future.

Jared's insight and expertise is utilized across a wide variety of sectors and industries from Fortune 500 companies to government municipalities, entrepreneurial start-ups, as well as some of his most recent work in Hollywood with accomplished actors, writers, and producers, helping them reinvent themselves and discover new areas for growth both inside and outside the bounds of their industry.

Jared is a national expert and delivers several keynotes and concurrent sessions throughout the year. Major trade associations, government entities, universities, and business development organizations regularly seek Jared out to deliver customized workshops and seminars that position their members for significant growth in the 21st century.

As a highly prolific author, Jared has published over 50 articles and is the author of Rethinking Reinvention, Leading the 21st Century: The CEO's Guide to Thriving in a Volatile and Uncertain Future, and Four Futures for the 21st Century Non-Profit. Jared is regularly quoted in the media on a wide variety of issues, which have included the future of entrepreneurship, the changing face of the news industry, capitalizing in uncertain times, the information economy, and the future of the workforce and education.

Jared is also a musician, composer, competitive cyclist, and trail runner living in Charlotte, North Carolina with his wife and their two sons.

PREFACE

Almost every week there's a report of some new disruption to our traditional paradigms of business and economics, social interaction, privacy, and our relationship with the natural environment.

When presented with such paradigm-shaking news, leaders of organizations often feel a sense of ambivalence due to the fact that they are ill-equipped to articulate the implications such things may have on their business or community. Many choose to ignore such things because there is little they feel can be done today that will make a significant difference. This often results in these organizations taking the default "business as usual" approach to future growth and success.

In order for us, as leaders and organizations, to create continuous growth despite increasing future uncertainty, we must rethink our concept and strategy for "growth."

For too long we've allowed the insane Wall Street model of quarterly earnings to dictate measures of growth in every market, sector, and industry. This one-dimensional focus on revenue growth has made it increasingly difficult for businesses to think beyond their present day situation and take action that positions them for long-term continuous growth. If we solely focus on growing revenue, then our efforts will almost certainly replicate what has worked well for past growth, without considering whether or not it will have the same outcome for future growth.

As leaders it's imperative we take a long-term view of growth and refocus the energy we expend trying to slow down or avoid disruptions and use it to create our own. Now more than ever we need to look beyond our next quarter profits and begin rethinking our next quarter century.

Jared Nichols
Principal – The Jared Nichols Group

INTRODUCTION

"The future never arrives. If it did, it would no longer be the future, but the present day. The future is always out in front of you, waiting to be created."

If you are reading this now it is because you are well aware that the world is changing at a rapid pace. The struggle to keep up and remain relevant becomes increasingly difficult by the day. For most, this situation is a continuous cause of stress and anxiety as they repeat the same processes for planning despite knowing the return is limited and likely to diminish in short order.

In conversations with clients and executives across the industry spectrum the same concern continues to arise, which is the need to prepare for and anticipate change long before it arrives. Traditional strategic planning and forecasting models have lost their prestige due to the fact that they were designed with the assumption that very little will change over the next one to five years. These models were designed under the premise of relative certainty and likely scenarios.

There wasn't much risk involved in these plans.

Trying to apply the same old model to today's business environment does not work. The battle for relevance and growth requires a deep futures strategy that enables an organization to anticipate disruption and shifts in the market and public policy. Leaders need a process that is both applicable and adaptable to sudden or unexpected changes.

This book will not teach you to predict the future, but rather how to create multiple future possibilities by which you can ensure your organization is set up to thrive regardless of the outcome.

As you begin, you must be prepared to do three things:

1. Challenge the traditional ideas about the future.
2. Challenge your own biases and assumptions about the future.
3. Challenge traditional models of decision making.

CHALLENGING TRADITIONAL IDEAS ABOUT THE FUTURE

Thinking about the future for some is seen as an exercise in futility due to the fact that the future cannot be fully known. But this is where the mindset must change in order to begin creating the future that will enable you and your organization to continue to grow and thrive over the next 5 to 25 years.

I've had the opportunity to work with some incredible organizations through this process and without fail, each of them have identified new areas for market and revenue growth. The same is possible for you reading this now. Consider the following:

The future never arrives. If it did, it would no longer be the future, but the present day. The future is always out in front of you, waiting to be created.

If you choose to undertake this endeavor, you will be required to rethink what is possible and allow yourself and your team to entertain absurd notions about the future. Impeding this process will limit your potential and prospects for dramatic growth. This is not to say that structure and parameters will be removed. Far from it. You will learn how to create highly focused objectives around critical questions that need answering.

CHALLENGING YOUR OWN BIASES AND ASSUMPTIONS ABOUT THE FUTURE

It's much easier to deny the possibility that a certain event (no matter how far-fetched) will actually occur or that an emerging trend that could drastically alter the business landscape will take hold. Unfortunately this is the position that the majority of businesses, organizations, and industries take in the face of potential disruption.

> For example, the "sharing economy" as it has come to be known, has been driven by consumers' desire to lease or share their property rather than buy or sell. Air BnB and Uber are just two examples that have disrupted long-standing industries that were so rooted in the belief that these concepts could never gain enough steam to truly be a threat. Well, they were wrong, and now they are fighting tooth and nail against a tide that does not look to be turning anytime soon.

Your long-term success requires that you pay attention to what is on the horizon as well as what is in front of you. If you focus too far out, you'll neglect important actions that need to be taken today. If you only focus on the present, then you will continue to be caught off guard and forced to maintain a reactive posture going forward.

CHALLENGE THE TRADITIONAL MODELS OF DECISION MAKING

Today, as in the past, we tend to make decisions based on the following:

1. Access to information
2. Interpretation of that information
3. Integration of that information into our cultural narrative

Now here is where the the past and present part ways.

In the past we had:

1. Limited or delayed access to information, which then led to a...
2. Narrower interpretation of that information, allowing for an...
3. Easier integration of that information into the cultural narrative ("good", "bad", "enemy", "ally")

As such, it was easier to make top-down decisions. Information was privileged and required a hierarchy in order to access it.

Consider our education system. We move up in grades, wherein we obtain new information handed down to us from our teachers and professors. The higher up you go, the greater the chances for mobility and long-term success. This is why expertise and the title of Ph.D have been synonymous in our culture for so long. But now we live in the Information Age, which has put a direct challenge to the traditional hierarchy of education whose value was heavily dependent on granting access to information.

Today we have:

1. Unprecedented and immediate access to information, which creates...
2. Multiple interpretations of that information, leading to...
3. A disjointed integration of that information into our cultural narrative ("good", "bad", "enemy", and "ally" all at the same time)

It is this same dilemma that leaders in business and organizations face today.

The primary objectives of this book will equip you to:

1. Leverage the unprecedented access we have to information today.
2. Create a contextual framework in order to better interpret that information.
3. Integrate that information into a powerful narrative that moves your people to action.

Now is the time to begin creating your future, because if you do not, someone else surely will.

PART ONE

ANTICIPATING THE FUTURE(S)

"There are known knowns. These are things we know that we know. There are known unknowns. That is to say, there are things that we know we don't know. But there are also unknown unknowns. There are things we don't know we don't know."

— Donald Rumsfeld, Former U.S. Secretary of Defense

FROM REACTIVE TO PROACTIVE

A common objective that my clients and prospective clients share with me is the desire to move from reactive to proactive. The obvious dilemma for many of them is that old methods of strategic planning do not prepare them for the unknown. Furthermore, if the future cannot be known, then how can we be proactive? We can start by leveraging our unprecedented access to information.

In order to determine which information we can use to be proactive and which we must simply react to, it is useful to group information into the following stages:

Stage 1: Weak Signal
Stage 2: Potential Event
Stage 3: Actual Event

Weak Signal Stage: This is when there are clues of an emerging trend, issue, or event that is far enough out that leaders, organizations, and communities have time to take proper action to prepare for or capitalize on that change. Weak signals are not guarantees that certain issues, trends, or events will occur. Instead, weak signals should be monitored to give you and your organization enough lead time to take incremental steps to prepare you for success if those changes, disruptions, or shifts do occur.

Potential Event Stage: This is when a likely event has not yet occurred and few are aware of it's potential. What makes this stage of information important is that its likelihood of occurrence is typically treated with skepticism and a "wait and see" response, since the implications are unknown and speculative at best.

Actual Event Stage: This is where information has become news and it is at this stage where the majority of people make their decisions. The obvious problem here is that there is only one option at this stage and that is to react.

Being proactive requires you to make preliminary decisions and take incremental actions beginning in Stage 1 or early Stage 2. In doing so, you might need to reframe your relationship with uncertainty and how you view the unknown. The fact that the future is unknown is an advantage to you for two reasons:

1. It levels the playing field. The unknown future is unknown to everyone else as well.
2. It gives you and your organization enough lead time to begin planning for multiple possibilities rather than waiting for some pre-determined inevitability.

ENSURING FUTURE RELEVANCE

I ask my clients the following three questions about where they are today:

1. What distinguishes your business from the competition?
2. What specific needs, issues, or obstacles is your business addressing?
3. What is the unique value that you bring to your clients, making you relevant in today's market?

Then, I ask them how confident they are that the factors that make them valuable today will still be relevant 5, 10, or 20 years in the future?

Without fail, the vast majority do not feel that the value they provide today would continue to be relevant in the future. Several of them feel that automation and technology are rapidly encroaching on both their market and their ability to distinguish themselves from the competition. One such example came from an attorney who specializes in succession and estate planning for closely held private companies. He talked about how social media such as the Youtube™ "How-To" videos and DIY companies like Legal Zoom™ are changing the way clients and prospective clients see the value that he provides.

This is why it is more important now than ever before to identify early signs of emerging shifts and changes that may drastically alter the business landscape and render your products and services irrelevant. Large and once prominent organizations such as Blockbuster, Circuit City, and Borders Books either failed to see the early warning signs or they chose to ignore them altogether. Once you're able to identify these early signs of disruption, you have the advantage and the opportunity to get out in front of these changes, positioning yourself and your organization for continued growth and future relevance. The key to successfully doing this is through exploring alternative future possibilities by uncovering the impacts and implications of emerging trends, issues, and potential events.

ESTABLISHING A FRAMEWORK

If we only look at how a certain technology, either one that is here today or one that is emerging, will impact the technology sector alone, then our perspective is far too narrow. In order to understand the real impact this technology may have on the future as a whole, we have to explore how this technology will affect other facets of society.

A perfect example of this is the role that social media (specifically Twitter and Facebook) played in the Arab Spring, effectively overthrowing a 30+ year dictatorship in Egypt. Most wouldn't have guessed that these new social media tools could have had such far-reaching political implications. This is why when we consider how a possible trend or event might shape the future, we must establish a framework that includes all aspects of society. A useful tool for doing this is the classification system known as S.T.E.E.P. (Social, Technological, Economic, Environmental, and Political).

Here is a brief summary of what each category includes:

Social - When we think about society, our definition tends to encompass most of the other categories. However, for the sake of categorizing and identifying specific trends, issues, and events within this category, we will look at how they impact social interaction, the way we relate to each other as people, and the opinions and inclinations that the public shares.

Technological - Because most people consider the future or foresight as centering on new technologies, the "technology" category may seem a bit redundant. However, despite technology becoming increasingly integrated into every facet of our lives, the advancement of or growth in the technology sector of our society is still very much vulnerable to outside trends, issues, and events.

Economic - Just as with most of these areas, you will see that several of the economic impacts may be interchangeable. For many of you the idea of "economic impact" is more familiar and a constant in the dialogue of our culture today. However, it is important to remember that the economic impact goes far beyond the effect that a trend, issue, or event has on the economy. When discussing the economic impact of a certain trend, issue, and event, we must think about specific areas where market confidence, financial stability, and access to capital are paramount to long-term growth and viability.

Environmental - Of all the different categories, environmental is the most important, because without the environment none of the other categories would actually exist. It is the category upon which all other categories depend; therefore, its impacts and implications are far-reaching. For example, extreme weather events are occurring more frequently, having a direct impact on the economy, our society, and the type of technology employed to respond.

Political – The political category centers on elected officials and governmental bodies that create and implement public policy. Key areas of focus in this realm include regulations, taxation, governance models, representation, and community engagement.

Put It to the Test:

Try this for yourself by identifying the S.T.E.E.P. impacts of Facebook™ and the social media revolution by listing 1 to 3 answers for each question. Each of the 5 questions represents one of the S.T.E.E.P. categories.

1. How have Facebook™ and the social media revolution created/eliminated/prevented criminals and criminal activity?
2. How have Facebook™ and the social media revolution impacted the way we consume media and report information?
3. How have Facebook™ and the social media revolution impacted our access to, the quality of, and the perceived value of education?
4. How have Facebook™ and the social media revolution impacted the quality of our food, food distribution systems, farming, and the agricultural industry as a whole?
5. What regulatory impact has Facebook™ and the social media revolution had on business and community growth and development?

SCANNING

When I've worked with company executives through my Executive Foresight Program* the one area where we tend to spend the majority of our time is environmental and horizon scanning. Each executive, regardless of company size and industry, has been stunned by the degree of information uncovered that could have tremendous impacts on their business. Many feel they need to spend the extra time here to catch up to the present day in order to accelerate and get ahead of potential shifts and changes coming down the road. Before we go into the specifics of environmental and horizon scanning, let's briefly discuss what scanning is.

Scanning is a process of looking for specific points of data, information, or resources that help to inform us of emerging trends, issues, or possible events. Too many people rely on a single media outlet, such as a specific cable news channel or news journal, as their sole source for news and information. What I have found in my own research and inquiry is that by the time these sources report on a trend or actual event in any facet of society, it is far too late to be proactive.

This is why it is increasingly important, especially in our age of information, for leaders and organizations to be skilled in the practice of scanning. They need to know how to search for and find clues of emerging shifts and changes, both within their industry or sector and beyond. There are two types of scanning that we will discuss, both of which are critical for success when planning for the future:

1) Environmental scanning is a process of looking for clues and information about sudden changes or emerging trends and issues within your industry or sector. Those things which have a direct or immediate impact on the future of your business, industry, and sector. This form of scanning is often more deliberate and purposeful, specifically looking for information around a certain issue or topic that is relevant to your business or industry.

2) Horizon scanning is a process of looking beyond the bounds of your industry, business, or sector, in order to gain greater insight into those things that may not have a direct and immediate impact on you and your organization but could have significant implications for the overall future.

Scanning will produce a vast array of information that has the potential to both excite or intimidate. The following process will help you narrow your focus and avoid becoming overwhelmed by the degree of information out there.

JARED'S 3 STEP PROCESS FOR SCANNING

Scanning can take on several forms, but to start out it is helpful to have a few formal guidelines to ensure that your efforts are maximized. I've developed the following process to help you and your team make the most of your time and quickly identify what is of greatest importance to you.

Step one: Identify an issue or critical question in order to establish the framework for your scanning efforts. Select an existing trend, current issue, or actual event where the full implications are not yet known.

For Example: Let's imagine we are in the entertainment industry and the issue we would like to explore further is the growing market for autonomous technology (artificial intelligence, robotics, drones, etc.).

First, we would formulate a question such as:

"How will the recent growth in autonomous technologies impact future growth for the entertainment industry?"

Step two: Identify the "baseline assumption" answer to this question. We do this by posing and answering a question like:

"What do the majority of my colleagues and industry experts have to say about this?"

Step three: Find information that either confirms or contradicts the baseline assumptions being made or creates a new assumption altogether.

It's important to note that scanning is both deliberate and accidental. Deliberate scanning is what we are discussing here. Accidental scanning happens when you're watching a movie, reading a book, listening to a podcast, radio show, or a lecture where something is said or new information is presented that piques your curiosity. The more you are deliberate with your scanning efforts, the more this becomes a naturally occurring practice in your everyday life. We are constantly taking in new bits of information both consciously and subconsciously. Knowing what to do with that information is where most get hung up and the brain stores it away in a drawer labeled, "Irrelevant." With practice, you will begin to train your brain to make sense of seemingly unrelated points of information and translate them into a relevant and applicable narrative to guide your strategic planning process.

THROUGH THE EYES OF A CHILD: THE SECRET TO SHAPING THE FUTURE

My four year old son keeps the whole family entertained with constant chatter about trucks, meteors, construction sites, pirates, dragons, etc. When my son finds a new interest whether it's Transformers or deep sea exploration, he is able to incorporate that new element right into the ongoing imaginative narrative he has constructed. It doesn't matter if he's building blocks or outside playing in the dirt, each new object and concept becomes part of his magical world of giant school buses, sandbox volcanos, super hero action figures, and sidewalk chalk supermassive black holes.

As adults, we often feel less capable of incorporating seemingly unrelated ideas and information into the ongoing narrative we have constructed throughout our lives. Out of necessity we establish rules and guidelines for how to think and feel about the new information that crosses our paths. We often find it most expedient to simply put these thoughts and ideas out of our heads in an attempt to maintain status quo.

The greatest advantage of living in the Information Age is also the greatest disadvantage, namely that we have so much information at our fingertips. Having this much information should make us more informed, less hindered, and free to challenge old beliefs and ideas. Unfortunately, for many the opposite is true. With so much information constantly challenging our personal, social, and political narratives, we have become more hindered, rigid, suspicious, fearful, withdrawn, or just overwhelmed. Creating your long-term successful future will require you to think more like a child and embrace the following:

1. A deep sense of curiosity
2. A willingness to constantly discover and be challenged by new information
3. The understanding that what we know is subject to change as new information is introduced

It is how we process and adapt that information that determines how we grow, evolve, and reinvent ourselves today and into the future.

For more information about Jared's Executive Foresight Program, go to thejarednicholsgroup.com/services/executive-foresight-development/

PART TWO

APPLYING THE FUTURE TO THE PRESENT DAY

"You must give yourself permission to consider the absurd, seemingly impossible, and at times, the utterly ridiculous, in order to strengthen your ability to plan for long-term success."

LEVERAGING THE FUTURE

Anticipating and applying the future to your organization requires you to take the information gained from scanning the environment and horizon and extrapolate the possible implications it will have on the future as a whole. The value of anticipating change is the ability to apply that information to our next actions. This involves learning the skills and methods necessary to develop alternative future scenarios and frameworks that challenge baseline assumptions and industry bias. Too many organizations look for clues about the future by staying within the bounds of industry forecasts and bias.

A recent Gallup-Lumina Foundation poll on the public's perception of higher education found that 96% of college and university chief academic officers were extremely or somewhat confident in their institution's ability to equip students for success in the workforce. At the same time only 11% of business leaders strongly agreed that college graduates were equipped with the skill sets and competencies required to meet the needs of their organizations.

When organizations solely rely on the internal industry expertise, they run headlong into the future with a false sense of security. Industry expertise is important, but the future of your industry and organization is dependent upon the future context within which it will operate.

CONTEXT IS EVERYTHING

The 21st century is changing the way we think about familiar concepts and terminology. For example, the term "hacker" had a predominately negative connotation until the early and mid 2000's. Now there are widely publicized hacker conferences and competitions. In fact, when I was choosing the name for my weekly newsletter "Hacking Your Future," I discovered a clear generational divide between those who associated the name with accessing valuable information for their future and those who associated "hacking" with gross invasion of privacy and criminal activity. This is but one example of how concepts that once held a widely agreed upon definition have drastically changed. Why exactly is that? The short answer is: context. Context defines concepts and will therefore also determine a consumer's changing perception of a particular product or service.

Businesses, products, services, and institutions lose relevance because they have either ignored or miscalculated changes to the business and social context. Consider the popularity of the "value menus" and "value meals" in the late 20th and early 21st centuries. These meals were low cost, low quality, and fast. The reason this concept was so successful was that it met a short-term need for food at a price point that outweighed the long-term cost to one's health. Consumer context in the last several years has changed dramatically.

The concept of value today is defined by both the short and long-term costs to the consumer, as consumer awareness about the quality of food and its impact on one's health increases. This shift in the consumer perception of value is causing industry leaders like McDonald's to make drastic decisions about their future direction and the action they must take to ensure their future relevance.

This is why leaders and organizations must be able to construct plausible future frameworks through available information, allowing them to detect early signs of dramatic change in order to take action before those changes occur. The concepts that currently define their businesses are sure to take on new meanings in future contexts. If a company, product, or service wants to continue to be perceived as having "value," it must determine what is likely to be perceived as valuable in the future.

On a side note...

We all have biases and we always will. There is nothing wrong with that as it's part of being human. Problems arise when we refuse to challenge those biases and assumptions and allow them to guide our decisions and dictate what is truly important and relevant with no regard to new information and ideas.

UNCOVERING POTENTIAL IMPACTS AND IMPLICATIONS

On several occasions I've been asked to run workshops that help individuals to think differently and more strategically about the future. One of the greatest challenges that leaders have when it comes to thinking strategically about the future is determining how to address large scale issues within the context of their businesses, organizations, and local communities. Too often the voices we hear addressing these complex issues tend to oversimplify them because that approach is easier and often more palatable to the public. Unfortunately, this does nothing to address the real issues each business, community, and organization faces as it looks forward.

I recently asked a group of community leaders what the greatest areas of concern about the future were for them. The following are just a few of the answers they gave:

* Prosperity at the expense of personal freedoms
* Loss of privacy and anonymity
* Decrease in communication and genuine human interaction
* Resource scarcity and sustainability
* Rising popularity of extremism
* Partisan politics impeding progress
* Surmounting student loan debt and employability of the younger generation

For many, these concerns often seem too far beyond their grasp to address, so instead they focus on the many seemingly "urgent" issues that are continuously popping up. The irony here is that these numerous tedious issues often result from the larger scale issues they feel unequipped to address. In order for leaders to address large scale concerns and the potential implications those issues may have on their businesses, organizations, and communities, they must push beyond the bounds of what they think is realistic or possible about the future and, more importantly, what they believe is possible about their role in creating their ideal future.

I emphasize this point when working with teams or running a workshop:

You must give yourself permission to consider the absurd, seemingly impossible, and at times, the utterly ridiculous, in order to strengthen your ability to plan for long-term success.

Just to drive this point home even more I want you to look at the image below. This photograph was taken in Fredericksburg, Virginia, after the Battle of Spotsylvania in 1864.

Photo courtesy of wikimedia commons

I want you to imagine sitting down with the men in this photograph and trying to explain drone technology, iPads, genetic modification, artificial intelligence, etc. The point here is that you would sound like a raving lunatic. What we know is possible today would have well exceeded their wildest imaginations about what was possible in the future.

Put It to the Test:

Pick any trend, issue, or potential event where the full implications are not known and little has been written about the impact it may have on your business, industry, or sector. Sample topics might include artificial intelligence, genetic modification, natural resource depletion, alternative energies, etc. The next step is to determine how your selected trend, issue, or event, may impact multiple facets of society. This is how you create context in order to determine the areas that are most critical for your business and organization. The following questions will help to get you moving in the right direction.

Social Implications:

How might_____ impact our traditional concepts of the family (social significance, roles within, etc.)?

How might _____ impact the arts and entertainment and our outlets for leisurely activities?

What new vices might come about as a result of _____ being introduced into our society?

How might _____ create/eliminate/prevent criminals and criminal activity?

How might_____ redefine/magnify/deteriorate our traditional concepts of community (local and national)?

Technological Implications:

How might _____ impact the way we communicate with each other and share our thoughts, ideas, and interests?

How might _____ impact the way we consume media and report information?

How might _____ impact our means of transportation and physical mobility?

How might _____ redefine/magnify/deteriorate our local and national ideas, concepts of community, as well as it's importance?

Economic Implications:

How might _____ impact discretionary income, private investment, and consumer spending?

How might _____ impact the demand for human labor, specialized skill sets, and talent?

How might _____ impact our access to, the quality of, and the perceived value of education?

How might _____ impact our currency on a national and global level?

Environmental Implications:

What impact might _____ have on the quality of our natural resources?

How might _____ impact the quantity of resources available to us today and in the future?

How might _____ impact the quality of our food, distribution systems, farming, and the agricultural industry as a whole?

What impact might _____ have on the preservation/protection/destruction of wildlife and biodiversity?

Political Implications:

What regulatory impact might _____ have on business and community growth and development?

How might _____ impact taxation and revenue generation, both at the local and national levels?

How might _____ impact the way in which we are governed?

How might _____ impact the way we engage with, and are engaged by, our government, politicians, and public servants?

DETERMINING IMPACT AND UNCERTAINTY

Once you and your team have uncovered the potential implications of your selected trends, issues, and/or events, the next step is to determine which implications have the greatest potential impact (positive or negative) along with the greatest degree of uncertainty. Now this may seem counterintuitive, but we want to focus on the greatest degree of uncertainty because such an issue or event is still far enough out in the future to take meaningful action today.

Too many organizations focus on high impact/high certainty events because they want to know how to best react to or recover from dramatic shifts and disruption. But if you want to be more proactive and create your future rather than react to it, then you need to reverse this thinking. Being prepared to identify, or even create, opportunities in areas of high uncertainty allows you to become the disruptive organization.

What It Means to Be "Proactive"

During an interview on *60 Minutes* Jeff Bezos was asked to comment on the criticism that his company, Amazon, ruthlessly puts small businesses in a position where they cannot compete. While some may view his manner as callous, his response was direct and honest, "Amazon is not happening to these businesses. The future is." Jeff Bezos' success is the direct result of his refusal to conform to "business as usual." Instead he chose a path that matched the emerging business landscape, disrupting the older business models.

Engaging in market disruption requires a long-term outlook and the ability to identify where opportunities for capitalization may emerge. Companies like Google, Samsung, Amazon, Shell Energy, and Apple consistently look at how the future may unfold over the next 25 to 50 years in order to take advantage of, or create their own, shifts in the market. They do this by focusing on emerging trends, issues, and potential events that have a high degree of uncertainty (many years down the road), but would have a tremendous impact on their business if they were to make no changes moving forward.

NARROWING YOUR FOCUS: HOW TO RANK IMPACT AND UNCERTAINTY

The overall purpose of this exercise is to help you establish your business and industry's most pressing issues and questions to address in order to ensure its long-term success. The questions that you were asked to answer in each of the STEEP categories identified potential implications and areas of uncertainty. Go back through your answers and create a simple statement that sums up the implications you found under each category.

<u>Example:</u>

Let's build on the previous example used in our discussion about scanning: "the commercialization of drones." We would look at the specific answers to the STEEP questions in the previous section in order to formulate a statement about this event's potential impact on a specific industry. For this example, we will look at how commercial drones might impact the arts and entertainment industry. To do so, we would look at the second question under the Social category, which asked:

"How might commercial drones impact the arts and entertainment industry and our outlets for leisurely activities?"

Our answers may look something like this:

A. <u>From an entertainment perspective</u> - Our current obsession with reality television and just-in-time entertainment could be accelerated by the use of autonomous drones, relaying actual real-life situations, responses, and personalities back to the viewing public.

B. <u>From a leisurely activities perspective</u> – Commercial drones could lead to vicarious tourism, creating seemingly authentic experiences without leaving the comfort of your own home. This could bring about a new market for vicarious drones relaying real-time sites, smells, sounds, and touch directly to the users through sensory technology in the form of a body suit or some other type of neurological connection.

We would then formulate an implication statement relevant to the industry, such as:

"Autonomous drones redefine reality television."

Next, we would decide the level of impact this would have on our industry, ranking our own estimation of the impact on a scale of 1 to 3.

1 = little to no impact

2 = some impact

3 = high impact

For the sake of this example, we would rank the degree of impact at a "3," much like the impact that YouTube™ has had on the entertainment industry.

Our next objective is to determine the degree of uncertainty surrounding this statement, ranking our own estimation of the degree of uncertainty on a scale of 1 to 3.

1 = little to no uncertainty

2 = some uncertainty

3 = high uncertainty

For the sake of this example, we would rank the degree of uncertainty at a "3," since, at this time, there are several obstacles that would need to be overcome for this statement to occur (FAA regulations, constitutional rights, privacy, etc.).

Use the template on the next page to organize and rank your implications in each of the STEEP categories.

S.T.E.E.P. IMPLICATIONS

Rank each implication on a scale from 1 (little to none) to 3 (very high).

SOCIAL IMPLICATIONS	IMPACT			UNCERTAINTY		
1	1	2	3	1	2	3
2	1	2	3	1	2	3
3	1	2	3	1	2	3

TECHNOLOGICAL IMPLICATIONS	IMPACT			UNCERTAINTY		
1	1	2	3	1	2	3
2	1	2	3	1	2	3
3	1	2	3	1	2	3

ECONOMIC IMPLICATIONS	IMPACT			UNCERTAINTY		
1	1	2	3	1	2	3
2	1	2	3	1	2	3
3	1	2	3	1	2	3

ENVIRONMENTAL IMPLICATIONS	IMPACT			UNCERTAINTY		
1	1	2	3	1	2	3
2	1	2	3	1	2	3
3	1	2	3	1	2	3

POLITICAL IMPLICATIONS	IMPACT			UNCERTAINTY		
1	1	2	3	1	2	3
2	1	2	3	1	2	3
3	1	2	3	1	2	3

Once you've organized and ranked impact and uncertainty the next step is to select the implication statements that are high impact/ high uncertainty. Again, you want to focus on these areas of high uncertainty as they provide the greatest degree of opportunity for being proactive. The statements you select will give you the basis for building alternative scenarios in the next section.

FORMULATING YOUR CRITICAL QUESTIONS

As you may have noticed, the recurring theme throughout this book is the need to think about the future as a spectrum of alternatives rather than a predetermined singular outcome. Everything we have discussed up to this point is for the purpose of creating a series of alternative future possibilities focused on one or two key areas of concern. The next step in this process is to formulate the "Will/Or" questions around the implication statements you've selected.

The following is an example of one set of "Will/Or" questions.

If we continue with our example of "autonomous drones redefine reality TV" for our "will/or" question, then our "will" question may look something like this:

Will the commercialization of autonomous drones create new market space for, and redefine our concept of, reality TV?

We can now establish the "or" question. The "or" question should be the alternative future scenario to the will question. In this example the alternative to the "will" question might be:

Or, will the FAA, privacy advocacy groups, and other regulatory bodies restrict the use of autonomous drones in the public sphere.

Once you have formulated your "Will/Or" questions, you have narrowed your focus to the areas of greatest concern to you. They also provide the basis for the alternative future scenarios against which you can measure your existing and proposed strategies for growth.

PART THREE

ADAPTING YOUR STRATEGY

Adaptation is the transformative process you and your organization will undergo after discovering how the principles of strategic foresight can be applied to your current and future situations. This is where you will build and implement strategies for several possible future outcomes that position your organization for success.

The first step in adaptation is creating a narrative on which to base the evolution of your business going forward. This is done through the process of scenario building.

SCENARIO BUILDING

The purpose of scenario building is to explore new ways of thinking about the future and how to apply the insights gained in this process to your present-day strategy. It is not about predicting the future. Scenario building and planning has been used both by major corporations such as Royal Dutch Shell and by the US military in order to make better, more informed decisions in the present. Having the ability to put all the information that you uncovered into a plausible and relevant narrative for the future of your industry and organization helps to ensure your adaptability to sudden shifts in the market, and your resilience in the face of unexpected events. The end result gives you a significant competitive advantage.

There are several ways to write a scenario. The method an organization chooses is heavily dependent on its objectives for the project at hand. Scenario building, planning, and implementation are typically done over several weeks with a team of individuals throughout the organization. The following is a simplified version of the scenario building process.

Refer back to the critical questions you have already formulated. Each of the "Will/Or" questions poses two alternative future scenarios. It would be beneficial to build a scenario for both potential outcomes of each critical question. Start by turning the question into a statement and base your scenario on the prospect that this statement does occur.

For example, "Will the commercialization of autonomous drones create new market space for, and redefine our concept of, reality TV?" becomes: "The commercialization of autonomous drones creates new market space for and redefines our concept of reality TV."

Place yourself 10 to 25 years into the future and imagine you are a historian recounting the events surrounding this phenomenon. The following questions will help you build context for your scenario as well as identify the obstacles and opportunities it presents.

JARED'S FIVE STEP PROCESS FOR SCENARIO BUILDING

Step one: What happened and when? - Start by choosing a timeframe that sets the stage for your scenario and fits with your chosen title.

Step two: How did it happen? Why? – What STEEP elements were present beforehand that played a key part in bringing this scenario to fruition? What indicators were present beforehand that, if addressed, could have prevented this scenario from taking place?

Step three: Who wins? Who loses? – Which segment of the population, age demographic, industry, sector, etc. came out ahead and which have suffered significant setbacks?

Step four: What did they do or not do? – What specific action did (or didn't) those who thrived in this scenario take to ensure their success?

Step five: Where are they now? – Where are both groups now? Are they thriving, suffering, or evolving? Why?

*A sample scenario based on the sample critical question and the process above is included in the appendix.

This process is complex and will stretch your creative and logical capacities to their limits. However, through practice, you will begin to adopt the principles of strategic foresight as a new way of thinking and taking in the world around you.

Let's review this process once more. You will use the critical questions you created, based on the implication statements that had the greatest degree of uncertainty and the greatest potential impact (meaning they also present the greatest opportunity). Each of these questions will be answered in the form of a story that you will write in order to gain a clearer picture of how this future scenario might look if it came to fruition. The five step process above will help you write this story. Keep in mind that each of the scenarios that you create should present a very different future outcome. Additionally, incorporating other trends that you uncovered through scanning into your narrative will make your scenario more effective. In doing so, you will have a much richer narrative, by which new points of information may emerge. This will give you greater insight into how to prepare for potential disruptors and transform them into new opportunities.

HOW FUTURE FIT IS YOUR ORGANIZATION?

So often we make recommendations for change, strategic initiatives, or tactical action, but fail to present a convincing argument to support our recommendations. By completing this process from scanning to scenario building, you now have the format to overcome that obstacle. You now have the ability to see the future as an array of possibilities, of which you can take an active role in shaping.

The next step is to measure your existing and proposed growth strategies against each of the alternative scenarios you have created. The key here is to determine which scenarios your proposed strategies are most compatible with and to determine what actions need to be taken against those scenarios for which your strategies are incompatible.

The scenario matrix is a simple tool you can use to rate your strategic compatibility. You will want to start by customizing the following matrix with the titles of each of your scenarios in the top horizontal row of boxes. In the vertical row on the left you will list up to five key company or industry strategies. You will then want to work through each scenario and strategy to determine how compatible the two are. Use the following key to color code each.

GREEN - Strategy is very compatible with scenario
YELLOW - Strategy is mostly compatible with scenario
RED - Strategy is not compatible with scenario

ALTERNATIVE FUTURE SCENARIOS

■				

STRATEGIES FOR FUTURE GROWTH

A sample completed matrix is included in the Appendix.

STRATEGIC RECOMMENDATIONS

For strategies scoring in the red, you should ask yourself the following questions:

1. What indicators should we watch out for that would signal this future scenario's likelihood?
2. What should we do today to ensure that we are prepared for this future scenario or one that is very similar to it?

For strategies scoring in the yellow, you should consider these questions:

1. Where do we need to focus our energy in order to ensure our future growth and long-term success?
2. What potential surprises lurking in this scenario should we be aware of?

START CREATING YOUR FUTURE TODAY

Once you've completed this process, you will be able to share with the members of your organization a clearer vision of the obstacles and opportunities ahead, ensuring their greater understanding of and investment in the direction of the organization. You will also be ready to use what you've learned to create a culture of strategic foresight and innovation within your organization. This is important because strategic foresight should never be considered a one-off process, but a new way of looking at the world. You will use these tools again and again to stay ahead of changes and create the future you want to see. As such, you will begin to build the kind of organization that employees want to work for and competitors strive to become.

Long-term continuous growth is possible, but not in the way that most traditional models portray. Continuous growth comes by way of ensuring that your products and services are relevant, designed, and redesigned to create long-term success for your target audience. Regardless of how uncertain, volatile, and unstable the 21st century may be, you have the power to create continuous success in your business and community. This will require you to be vigilant about what is on the horizon, scrutinize the data you use to make long-term strategic decisions, and be willing to take the necessary steps to ensure your work's success.

APPENDIX

PRACTICAL ADVICE FOR SCANNING

You will start by entering keywords into one of the many search engines such as Google, Bing, and Yahoo.

If your critical question was:

"How will the recent growth in autonomous technologies impact future growth for the entertainment industry?"

You would want to enter keywords and phrases such as:

"autonomous technology and the future of (your industry)"

Or, look for information that might shift, disrupt, or change autonomous technology.

Each scanning hit will need to be categorized according to its STEEP classification. Many of the scanning hits that you find can be classified under multiple STEEP categories.

You will also need to specify the type of scan hit. Use one of the four different types listed below.

Existing Event
Defined as:

1. An event that has already happened.
2. Its implications are not fully developed.
3. Very few people are aware this event has taken place.

Potential Event

Defined as:

1. Likely to happen or occur.
2. Implications are not fully known or understood.

Emerging Trend

Defined as:

1. Consistently surfacing over time.
2. Usually characterized by an increase or decrease of a particular area or thing.

Emerging Issue

Defined as:

1. Creating conflict or debate.
2. Requires a decision where the results will impact an industry or segment of the population.

The template on the next page will help you to categorize the information you uncover from your scanning efforts.

SCANNING TEMPLATE

Critical Question:
Baseline Answer / Assumption:

Existing Event____	Emerging Event____	Potential Event____	Emerging Issue____
Brief Description:	STEEP Category(s): Social____ Technological____ Economic____ Environmental____ Political____	Effect on Industry baseline: Confirms____ Contradicts____ Creates____	Impact on the Future: ____ *Rate on scale of 0-5 where 0 = little to no impact and 5 = disruptive/transformative*
In what way(s) does this impact the future of your industry/sector?			
Who is potentially impacted by this and why?	Name(s):	Why?	
Resulting new or confirmed scenario(s)			

Contributor:
Source:
URL/full citation:
Keywords:

"THE COMMERCIALIZATION OF AUTONOMOUS DRONES" IMPACT WHEEL EXAMPLE

The impact wheel is a visual tool we often use to make connections among the various S.T.E.E.P. categories. This is a stripped down representation of the process we used to establish potential impacts and implications.

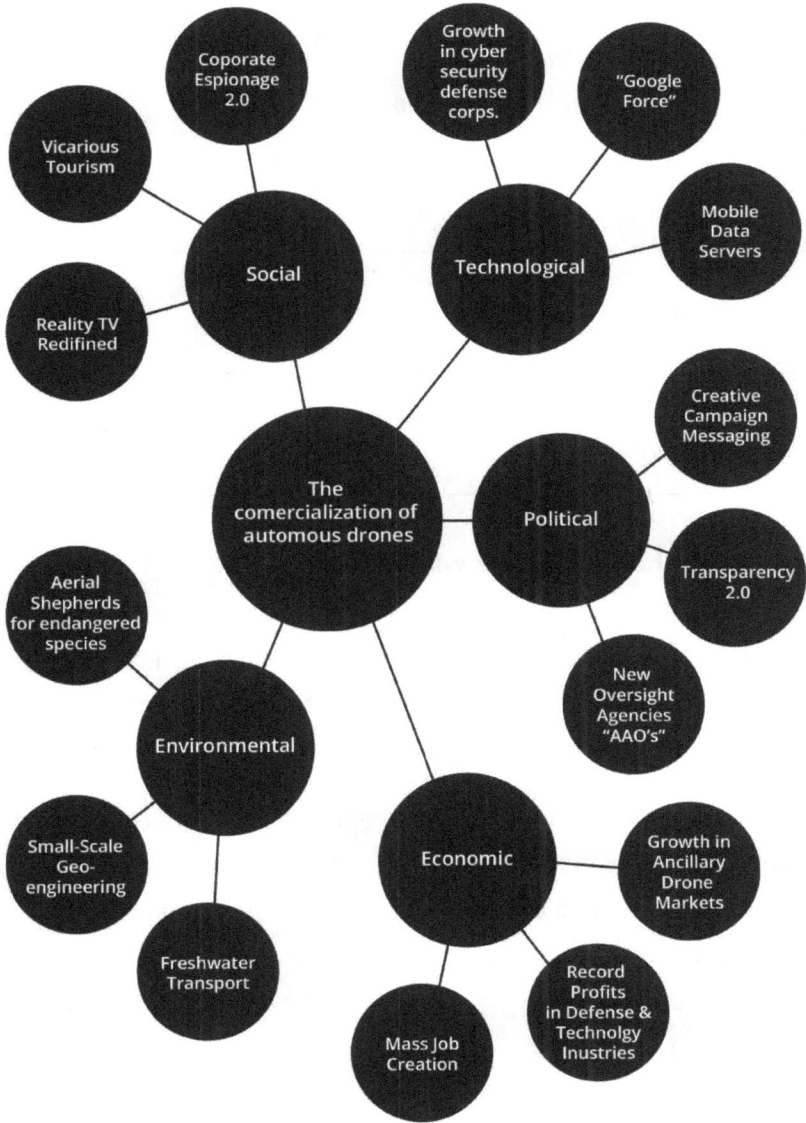

SCENARIO BUILDING TEMPLATE EXAMPLE

Below is the example I created and use for the Executive Foresight Development Program. Keep in mind that this example is the outcome of my scanning efforts so try not to let certain details distract you. It is a creative, but plausible, scenario based on current trends and potential future events.

"Will/Or" Question

> Will the commercialization of autonomous drones create new market space for, and redefine our concept of, reality TV?

Scenario Title and Date

> "The World is Watching"
> *August 15, 2035*

Step 1: What happened and when?

> **2019** - The FAA eased restrictions on the use of autonomous drones allowing individuals and corporations to purchase "air time" for the delivery of goods and services.
>
> The high cost of "air time" and the requirement that drones must meet strict FAA standards, helped to ensure a slow integration in what was sure to be an explosion in new market space.

Step 2: How did it happen and why?

2017 – The rise in personal and corporate cyber attacks over the past decade made way for tech giants like Google™, Facebook™ and Microsoft™ to partner with defense and aerospace corporations such as Northrup Grumman and Boeing to create a system of "moving data servers," paving the way for new market space in cyber defense security. This led to the gradual easing of FAA restrictions on the use of drones for commerce in 2019.

2021 - The U.S. Supreme Court rules that because the FAA has no regulatory authority on airspace under 400 feet, the oversight and regulation of commercial drones was out of their jurisdiction, opening the floodgates for public drone use.

2022 - The oversight of drone activity falls to the (DHS) Department of Homeland Security.

2023 – The DHS creates a special agency to oversee all ambiguous airspace operations, better known as, "AAO's."

Step 3: Who wins and who loses?

Wins

Aviation and Defense companies such as Boeing Co, Astrotech Corp, General Dynamics Corp, Lockheed Martin Corp, and Northrup Grumman Corp.

Tech Companies: Google™, Facebook™, Microsoft™, etc.,

The general public: Low cost/high tech brings new jobs, new experiences, new opportunities, new ways of interacting.

Loses

The general public: Privacy has been greatly diminished. Low cost/high tech is overseen by the DHS and data collection has become seen as a "necessary evil" because of the increased threat of cyber attack on individuals, corporations, and government agencies.

The entertainment industry: Accessibility to drones has redefined "reality tv" and steered profits away from the big production companies who now compete with their past consumer base. For the first time, "reality tv" is what it claims to be.

Corporations: "The world is watching" has created greater public oversight on the activities of corporations. Several companies now find themselves preoccupied with shareholder/stakeholder mediation instead of growth and increasing profits.

Step 4: What did they do or not do?

Aviation/Defense and the Tech giants quickly saw new market opportunity to fill a widening gap in cyber security and drive record profits. These industries had already worked together in the past on national security initiatives, so compatibility was not an issue.

Step 5: Where are they now?

Google Force (Defense R&D) is the highest grossing division of Google Inc. and the largest cyber defense contractor in the world.

Reality TV has evolved into a collaborative movement to solve the world's problems and create greater transparency and accountability among elected officials, corporations, and government entities.

SAMPLE SCENARIO MATRIX

The following is an example of a strategy matrix I used with a client in the non-profit sector. This matrix was specific to the organization rather than the industry.

ALTERNATIVE FUTURE SCENARIOS

INDUSTRY STRATEGIES FOR FUTURE GROWTH	The Forgotten Minority	The Conscious Economy	The Endangered Donor Demographic	Social Technology & The Resurgence of Human Innovation
Diversify Revenue Streams				
Adopt Strategic Social Media Initiatives				
Incorporate New ICT for fundraising				
Pioneer New Service Models as an Example for the Industry				
Create a long-term campaign to enlist private business as strategic partners				

NOTES

www.ingramcontent.com/pod-product-compliance
Lightning Source LLC
Chambersburg PA
CBHW070909210326
41521CB00010B/2114